Lifetime
Memories
in Verse

by

Joyce Johnson

FIRST EDITION

©opyright 2017 by Joyce Johnson

Edited by Gary Drury

ISBN-10: 1981640762
ISBN-13: 978-1981640768

Gary Drury Publisher™
Kentucky

Produced in The United States of America.

To Alice
I hope you enjoy
and think of me,
Love, Joyce

Table of Contents

Life & Family

The Perfect Age

If I could live my life again
I might wish to be twenty
When life and love still lay ahead
And dreams were mine aplenty.
Or it's probable that thirty
Would be just the age for me,
With my three children gathered
Round my still shapely knee.

Or could I live my life again
I might choose to be forty.
With cares of early childhood past,
I had time to look sporty,
But as I ponder on it,
Life was still great at fifty.
Free then to love myself a bit.
Yes, fifty would be nifty.

But since I can't go back in time,
I'll love the age I'm living;
Knowing the good Lord is my judge
And that He is forgiving.

Regrets

The green hills of my childhood
are calling me home.
I long to return and to
never more roam.
I still see the smoke from
my daddy's cigar
and feel Mom's last kiss as
I leave in my car.

The road has been winding for
seventy years;
how strange that so plainly I still
see their tears.
Is a light in the window still
burning for me?
They're no longer there so I
know it can't be.

Tears start to descend, but
I wipe them away
as I regret their sadness that
long ago day.

My Sickbed

I couldn't tell what he was saying
Standing there by my sick bed.
He was holding up a dollar.
As I tried to clear my head.

"We sheared all of the sheep today,
This dollar is for you.
Your lamb had such a nice thick coat
Of wool, the finest too."

I was nine years and never
Had a dollar for myself.
I watched him wink and tuck it
Very high upon the shelf.

I wondered what would happen
If it was I were to die.
Would my sister get my dollar?
I was much too sick to cry.

My mamma came with Jello and
A cool cloth for my head,
Saying softly, "You'll be well soon."
As I waited to be fed.

I don't remember how I spent it
That silver dollar of my own.
Perhaps I shared it with the others
Bought us each an ice cream cone.

But I remember Daddy as
He tried to make me smile,
And my mamma as she whispered.
"You'll be better, after while."

Mother's Tender care

Two times I had pneumonia,
Just to give my folks a scare.
Doctor's potions didn't cure me,
It was my mother's tender care.

We had all of the illnesses
That were around back then.
Measles , Mumps and Chicken Pox,
And the Scarlet Fever when

Quarantined for seven weeks,
One sick, one better, one well.
How our mother managed ,
I wish she were alive to tell.

A child crying because he hurt.
One whining he'd nothing to do,
Our loving mother's patience must
Have almost worn through.

We had no electronic games
No radio or TV and all.
What we did for entertainment
I truly can't recall.

Our mother came at every ring
Of our noisy bedside bell;
But she wouldn't let us read a book
Until completely well.

Measles sometimes weakened eyes;
Left my brother slightly deaf.
The doctor had the final word
But Mother was the ref.

We all survived these illnesses
Though doubtful, once or twice.
Mother claimed us worthy of
Her loving sacrifice.

Fighting On

Relentlessly the years go by.
Defensively I bravely try
To fight the ravages of time
As if it were an evil crime
To let the gray in dark hair show.

My beautician makes a brave attempt
To tidy up my poor unkempt
Tresses that have grown so thin;
Each day a task harder to win.
I should just act my age, I know.

But I am woman and I will
Take every potion, cream or pill
That promises beauty from ajar
To cover every little mar
And other signs of aging slow.

You would not recognize this face
If you saw it without a trace
Of makeup when I first awake;
And I don't even like to take
A look myself when age lines show.

So fie on you who'd ask my age.
To be so bold is an outrage.
Just let me have my bit of pride
My year of birth is classified.
I'm giving age the old heave-ho,
The lines and gray will have to go.

First-Born

There is something about a first-born
That claims a mother's heart
And breaks it into pieces
The day they have to part.

Oh, Lord I wasn't ready
To send him home to you
But when You said , "It's time to go",
What else was I to do?

Oh, there's something about a first-born
That cannot be replaced.
I loved him so, that he must go
Is the hardest thing I've faced.

Your mother knows the feeling.
She lost her first-born too
And now in Heaven's glory
She's living there with You.

He left me with Your promise
Some day we'll meet again
And when at last I hold him
I'll be freed of this pain.

Daddy's Day

On this one day we brought to you
A fancy cake, a tie or two.
You gave three sixty four to us
But always said we shouldn't fuss,
Nor waste our cash upon our dad.
We'd see you looking at an ad
For fishing tackle or a pole.
Your wish you would not tell a soul.
We'd pool our money and would buy.
The special gift that caught your eye.
Each child of yours knew he'd been blessed.
With better dad than all the rest.
We knew we'd never do enough
For he who in good times or tough,
Worked hard to make our lives a joy.
Earned the love of each girl and boy,
By always putting himself last.
I wish I could recall the past.
Now when money is not so tight.
It could be possible you might.
Buy what you never could afford.
That shiny, beautiful, new Ford.

Daddy you've gone to your reward
A goal we are still working toward.
In Heaven, Daddy, I know that you
Are doing what you used to do.
Still protecting your loved seven
Guiding us to you and Heaven.
Now all the others are there with you.
Someday I know, I'll be there too.

Daddy's Table

Just a little library table
Always in our living room.
With the bible that lay on it
It became a loved heirloom.

Grandma bought it for my daddy
Just to make his home less bare
When she visited Dakota
And his little homestead there.

Daddy loved that little table
And presented it with pride
To my mama when he married
His beloved and cherished bride.

Mama took care of that table,
Rubbed it to a lovely glow,
Giving it the place of honor
Because she loved my daddy so.

When our home was lost to fire
He made sure we were alive
Then rushed in to save the table
In the year of thirty-five.

Daddy died and then my mama
But the table still remains,
Relic of those days in history;
Homesteading on Dakota plains.

Cost a pittance when she bought it
In the year nineteen ought two
She'd be surprised at how we prize it,
If our grandma only knew.

Alone

Mama and Daddy and brothers,
And I the new baby adored,
Uncles and aunts and grandmothers,
It seemed I would never be bored.

Neighbors and friends and cousins,
All wanting to rock me a bit.
The very first girl in our family,
Was acknowledged a perfect fit.

A sister and brother would follow
To bring me companionship.
With abounding love surrounding
Surely life would be a grand trip.

I didn't foresee all the shadows
And the changes along the way,
Or that I'd be the oldest person
Alive in my world today.

They stayed until I was grown
Into a young woman and wife.
They thought they were no longer needed.
To guide me along in my life.

But oh what a lonesome feeling
That the first loved ones that you knew
Are gone to their Heavenly father
And there's nobody left but you.

When I Was Ten

Away back then, when I was ten,
Was truly a long time ago.
I was a child still running wild,
And of troubles, I didn't know.
World War One had been fought,
And our freedom bought,
When I was a child of ten.
With war to end all wars ended,
We'd never see war again.

Innocently, I laughed and played,
There was nothing of which I was afraid.
We played in the sun and we slid in the snow.
We liked to see our gardens grow
The year was Nineteen Twenty Eight,
When I swung so hard on the garden gate,
And laughed because I was finally ten
And would never be younger than ten again.

When Our three Children Were Small

I'd like to recall them
The songs I sung for them
When my three children were small.
I made up the lyrics, sometimes in hysterics
We'd laugh at the fun of it all..
They'd cuddle in bed then
After prayers and the Amen
Their daddy would come down the hall.
We'd give hugs and kisses
To our son and young misses
When our three children were small.

Pets Forever My Friends

Where is She?

Where is that cat? I look about.
I'm sure I didn't let her out.
I search the house once more again,
Not used to cold, she must stay in.
I open outside doors and call,
The cold wind enters, but that's all.
Is she outdoors, teasing a mouse?
She simply isn't in this house.

Turn off the lights, it's time for sleep,
But thoughts of her to my mind creep.
I visualize my frozen kitty.
I'll miss her so, it's such a pity.
Needing a blanket, I arise;
Open the closet, big surprise.
Deep in its depths, I see her where,
In perfect comfort, she lies there.
I carefully leave the door ajar.
"Okay, you stay right where you are."

Irreplaceable

You came to me in early spring,
A lost and sad, abandoned thing.
You were a lean and starving cat.
Choice nibblets soon took care of that.
Your true self emerged quickly and
You showed a preference for canned
Rather than dry food Blackie ate,
If offered on a china plate.
Your hair was long and silky now.
You taught Big Black to scrape and bow;
Your subject made to understand
You were the queen in full command.
You never walked across the floor,
Instead would leap counters before
Landing neatly at your full dish,
Haughtily giving tail a swish.
You challenged everything in sight.
All cats and dogs bewared your might.
Yours were the very sharpest claws.
You liked to show them just because.
Every chair and sofa was your throne.
My lap was yours and yours alone.
The dining table not exempt;
If you wanted, that is where you slept.
You ruled this place for four short years.
Now Blackie mourns and I'm in tears,
Last night you challenged just once more,
That fast descending garage door.
I found you very much too late.
You died beneath the heavy weight.
Why did this race you wish to choose?
Your little door was there to use.
You're buried in the comer lot.
I am so sorry I forgot

To check your whereabouts before
I sent that monster to the floor.
You purred your way into my heart;
Now my whole world is tom apart.
Another like you, I'll not find,
Miss Dinah, my one of a kind.

From my Point View

I wouldn't be so irritated
As I am when I find you
Have opened the door and walked right in,
If you would just shut it behind you!

A dog's life is really easy,
You needn't pay the monthly rent
Or worry about high prices.
With small things you are content.

I'm always at your beck and call.
You want in, then you want out.
You don't worry about escaping heat
And then wonder why I shout.

The first of April hasn't brought
The warmth of Spring this year.,
So we must both conserve a bit
Since fuel oil is so dear.

I know that all my fussing
Is falling on deaf ears
But life for me is not as soft
As in your eyes it appears.

The sun is shining brightly
And the grass is greening too
But Susie, I can't come out to play.
It's only thirty-two. (Fahrenheit that is.)

The Rides The Thing

Susie knows that we are going
Watching as I lock the door.
It's apparent by her actions
She can't wait a minute more.
Never mind our destination,
It's the ride that is the thing.
She wants the window to be open
Be it winter, fall or spring.
Eagerly she sticks her head out,
Barks at other dogs and bikes.
Doesn't ask, "When do we get there?"
It's the riding that she likes.
When I stop to run an errand
And I leave her in the car,
She doesn't worry, certain that I
Won't be gone too long nor far.
I leave all the windows open,
For I know no thief would dare
To attempt to steal our auto
With big Susie sitting there.

I found Susie at a no kill place,
Where she had been too long.
It was obvious that she'd been loved.
 But somehow her life went wrong.
For seven years this yellow lab
Was always at my call.
The empty places in my life,
She tried to fill them all.

Please give us some space aplenty
When we're heaving into sight.
This grandma and her aging dog
Are stepping out tonight.

With the windows all wide open
You might hear us as we sing,
"We don't care where we are going,
It's the riding that's the thing."

Uncertainty

It's 6:00 am Suzy, no need to get up.
I have turned ninety and you are no pup.
What is your hurry? Why not lie abed?
We've no pressing duties,
In this long day ahead.

Oh well, if I must, I will open the door.
You seem so eager to go and explore.
You want to know who has invaded your space,
As with nose down, you're running
All over the place.

The mouse who stole food from your dish has been caught,
Because he did something that he hadn't ought.
I only half-heartedly baited the trap.
I thought him a brave and quite
Cheeky young chap.

I accept as God's gift this new day that's begun
And look for some urgent, small tasks to be done.
With our breakfasts over and dishes washed too,
You're napping already
With nothing to do.

While I, as a human, am not made that way,
Though arising too early, awake I must stay.
For I know that summer is not here to last.
I must use it or lose it,
Time's moving so fast.

You think you're immortal, I know that I'm not.
This life I am living is all that I've got.
My life has been happy, I'd live it again,
But joys of today are
All filtered through pain.

I envy your living in only the now
I'd like to do that if I only knew how.
The lot of the human is living with fear
That as soon as tomorrow
She may not be here.

Aging Susie

My darling Susie cannot hear.
Is almost blind as well.
She finds her way around the yard
By her keen sense of smell.
She hasn't lost her appetite,
Seems to be feeling well.
I don't know if she's hurting
Because Susie doesn't tell.

She spends her day just sleeping
Until just before its dark
I let her out into the yard
To run around and bark.
She's made herself protector
Of me and this old place
And is warning all the wildlife
To stay out of our space.

She doesn't hear me call her name
So I turn on the light,
She sees and knows her job is done.
We're both safe for the night.
I let her out a while ago
To answer Nature's call.
I knew she wouldn't wander far
And worried not at all.

She sometimes takes a little swim
In the ditch across the way,
When it is full of water
But it is quite dry today.
Through the window I saw a car pull up
And its driver stepped outside.
He stood looking down into the ditch.
I ran out terrified.

Susie had decided to take a dip
Not knowing the ditch was dry.
She could not get up the slippery slope
No matter how hard she would try.
The stranger was trying to call her,
But of course she couldn't hear
And paid no attention to him
Until she sensed me near.

She let him take her collar then
And pull her the rest of the way.
She followed me back to the house.
With excitement enough for the day.

Christmas & Other Holidays

Thankfulness

The day has dawned both bright and clear
With lovely November weather
Another Thanksgiving day has come
When we can be together.

We're thankful for the blessings
That have been ours this year
And pray for the protection
Of all those we hold most dear.

We remember the hungry of the world
The homeless and the ill
And ask your blessing on them too
If this should be thy will.

Amen

A Christmas Snow

In our mild climate, we're more apt
To find a Christmas rose
Blooming in our garden,
Than any Christmas snows.

Yet some lucky years it happens
And the snow comes just in time
To cover up the fall's debris
And thus this little rhyme.

On Christmas Eve it started
In soft and fluffy fall.
We watch with delight the changes
As it covers over all.

Each flake is small and trifling
Yet joining with the others,
It becomes formidable and bold
And envelopes all with smothers.

The beauty over-powering
Under day or night time skies
Is a wonder world of pure delight
And a sight to mesmerize.

The Forgotten Veteran

They fought as bravely as the others.
When they were wounded, yes they bled.
They loved each other as if brothers.
And when they died were truly dead.

It was a quite unpopular war,
Our country's leaders were to blame.
It should not have been the soldiers who
Came home to silence, even shame.

Only their families welcomed them,
The lucky ones who came back home.
Their jobs were gone, their futures too.
Ill health and muddled minds for some.

If you meet a Viet Nam Veteran,
There are some words you need to say.
Please walk up to him, shake his hand
And thank him on this Memorial Day.

Remembrance Day

On this Memorial Day I bring
Bouquets to those I've known
Who have gone on to their rewards
With angels 'round His throne.

My mama and my daddy
My brothers, numbering five,
I loved them all so dearly
When they were still alive.

My husband and my precious son
My small granddaughter too,
If I must strip my garden bare,
It's little enough to do.

I'll wear a bright red poppy for
Some other mother's son
And sit with all my memories when
Remembrance Day is done.

Sleep My Child

Silent night, Holy night
Sleep my child until light.
God has sent Angels to you
To keep you safe the whole night through.
Sleep to my lullaby
Sleep to my lullaby

Christmas morn, Christmas morn
The Christ Child has been born
To bring the world sweet peace and love,
A Christmas gift from God above.
Praising God for his birth.
Praising God for His birth.

Letter to Santa

Dear Santa. I fear I've not always been good
Nor minded my mama as much as I should.
But I didn't mean it and if you will come
I'll leave you some cookies, some milk and some gum.

I pulled the cat's tail till he jumped and meowed,
And scratched my dear daddy who hollered aloud.
He said I would find an old rock in my sock,
But Mama said, "Hush, you're reacting to shock."

She suggested that I should just write you to say,
I'm sorry and I will try hard to obey.
I love you, dear Santa and if you forgive,
I'll carry the trash out each day that I live.

Don't listen to Sister who can't take a joke.
Could you bring her a doll for the one that I broke?
Tell my daddy you think I should have one more chance
And not do as he threatened to send me to France.

Love Suffices

It is buried rather deeply
In my far away recall,
The little paper Christmas tree
We had when I was small.
It had metal candle holders
On the end of each thin bough.
How it looked when it was lighted
I cannot remember now.
Perhaps one blaze of glory
With my daddy standing by
With a bucket full of water
If the flame should get too high.

A flash of recognition
When I saw it on the show
Of the antiques and mementos
From the years of long ago.
My brothers would remember
They're no longer here to ask,
But covering it with baubles
Would have been my mama's task.
I can see her bravely working
Barely holding back the tears
At the scarcity of presents
In those dark depression years.

With the love that was wrapped with them
I doubt we children ever knew
Gifts of that early Christmas
Were both trivial and few.

Holy Christ Child

Yes, I was there when he was born,
that all mankind from sin be shorn.
When his folks were told no room at inn,
kind creatures welcomed Him as kin.
The shepherds and the Magi came and
with great reverence praised His name.
A shepherd who dared not leave his sheep,
brought them along the Babe to meet.
I watched the scene with pure delight,
knowing I'd shared with all that night.
I am the cow who led her calf
without a herdsman with his staff.
I left a stall still warm but bare
for that sweet Child and his natal care.
Sweet Mary smiled her thanks to me.
That she was tired was plain to see.
When the child was born the angels sang.
and unseen bells with gladness rang.
There was no rest for man nor beast.
Many came the best and least.
Their respite was challenged the next morn
when rumors flew "A king was born".
Herod was consumed with rage,
when he was told this by a sage.
He decreed that all boys under two,
must die, and then to prove it true
and he wasn't just having a bit of fun
he even murdered his own son.
The family fled with their new son
and though many terrible deeds were done,
this child was saved and lived to be
savior of humanity.

Emma

No one should die on Christmas,
That happiest time of the year.
You know we love her Jesus
And want to keep her here.

She has heard you calling
And has answered to her name
But don't take her on Christmas
If it is all the same.

I know you'll do what's best, Lord
 But we have loved her so,
And any day but Christmas
We'll agree to let her go.

We've prayed that she could stay, Lord,
But that is not to be.
The doctors say this Christmas is
The last she'll ever see.

We could not give her up, Lord
This child beyond compare,
If we were not so certain
That you will meet her there.

Please have the angels waiting
To stay close by her side.
And even if its Christmas
By your will we abide.

She didn't die on Christmas, Lord
In answer to our prayer.
To let her go at Christmas time
We thought we could not bear.

She stayed with us through winter
And watched with us for spring.
It was in the last days of July
She left on Angel's wing.

This Christmas will be lonely Lord
Our Emma won't be here,
We're so thankful that you let her stay
Through Christmas time last year.

We made a few more memories,
Though some were bitter/sweet,
We pray enough to last until
In your own time we meet.

Christmas is Coming

Christmas is coming and I have been good
Or at least, Dear Santa, as good as I could.
I helped with the baby and tied Johnny's shoes
I got 'A' on my paper, is that not good news?

I know Johnny tries, but sometimes he forgets
That Christmas is coming and has temper fits.
If you've given his gifts to the good little boys
Please take some of mine, for he must have toys,

To open on Christmas or I will be sad,,
He's my brother, I love him, if he's good or he's bad.
Don't give him my doll, for that would be folly.
He'd just break its head as he did my old dolly.

Christmas Week Jitters

"It's Christmas Week and I'm not ready",
Is that what Mary said
When she found herself in Bethlehem
No place to rest her head?

I ponder this as I lament.
"The power was out for days.
I was snowbound the week before.
The rain just stays and stays.

How can I get my shopping done?
I have more fudge to make
The leaves, the howling wind brought down,
Await me and the rake."

Christmas Eve is coming soon.
I'm really in a tizzy.
The clock hands spin around so fast,
They leave me feeling dizzy.

Just as sheer panic starts to reign,
I give myself a shaking.
I'll tackle one task at a time,
The cleaning and the baking.

Just as sweet Mary calmed herself
For this Child she soon adored,
Christmas Eve will find me ready
For the birthday of my Lord.

Christmas Wishes

Peace for the world the tidings brought
And love for all the message taught;
And that my self same wish today
For loved ones near or far away.

The world's most precious Christmas wish
Was served up then in one small dish;
The precious Child that Mary bore
To bring us peace forever more.

There is no way that I can say
It better than they this Christmas day.
Peace and Goodwill and Love to you,
My loved ones, Nation and World too.

A Tale Oft Retold

The glorious Christmas music
Rings out o'er all the earth
Proclaiming and exulting in
The precious Savior's birth.

In every language every mode
The Christmas tale is told
And it is just as new to some
As in those days of old.

Each year our pastor takes a rest
And lets the children tell
The story of the Baby's birth.
Small voices tell it well.

The little children in their robes
Sing of the Heavenly King
As did the angels long ago
The happy tidings bring

My flagging Christmas spirit
Has been refreshed today,
By the singing of the children in
Their little Christmas play.

Palm Sunday

A million prayers beat on Your ears.
You wiped a thousand million tears.
And sent Your angels to protect
The seven we did not expect
To see again this side of Heaven.
Then You returned our beloved seven

We awakened on this Palm Sunday;
Our thoughts 2000 years away.
To time when You were facing death
 Blessing this world with dying breath.
Today once more the palm leaves wave.
In knowledge that our God can save.

From triumph to that black Friday
We follow as you wend your way.
Suffering your every wound and blow,
We walk with you as on you go,
From dark despair to greatest glory
Our soldiers too, an Easter story..

Their suffering we don't yet know,
But somehow we felt every blow.
The lesson taught so long ago
Is happiness can follow woe,
If we remember God is King
And triumphs over every thing.

Please change our enemies to friends
And guide us as this wartime ends.
May Easter bring the joy of peace,
Our love for You and man increase.
Let us not in happiness forget.
The many who are sorrowing yet.

We've proven we're the side with might.
Keep us also on the side that's right.

Nature

Spring Wealth (abecedarian)

Azaleas putting on spring frocks of
Beautiful shades of salmon or pink,
Calling bees to pollinate
Delighting humming birds with drink.
Everything is new in spring.
Fruit trees gorgeously attired.
Gardens turning up their soil,
Hoping we will be inspired.
I am the happiest of all,
Joyful with the sights and sounds,
Kerchief covering my hair,
Lifting plants and planting mounds.
Many birds are building nests,
Nature is budding everywhere.
Outdoors calls me, rain or shine,
Peonies with loveliness to spare.
Quite a magic sight to see,
Resulting in an outdoor room
Sumptuous and magnificent,
The whole of Nature is in bloom.
Utter saturation of color with
Violets peeping through at me.
What a lovely sight they are,
Xaggerated to the nth degree.
Yes the beauty there to see
Zaps my heart and sets it free.

Wild Lupines

High in the Alpine meadow
As flat on my back I lie,
My privacy is absolute,
Surrounded by the sky.
The blue lupines around me
In wild abandon grow.
Loveliness so unearthly
Must be Heaven's over-flow.
Sole food for the blue butterfly
Lupines survive the winds
And snows of mountain meadow
Until the winter ends.
God gives them everything they need
To live their short life span,
The lovely flower and the butterfly,
Far from the eyes of man.

Tulip Mania

The winter weary worshipers
Of beauty, wend their way
Through the bright array of tulips
That have opened up today.
Spring has been late and cold and
The flowers hid their heads.
The late snows and the rains could not
Entice them from their beds.

The laggard sun has come today
To show his mighty power.
He coaxed the petals to unfurl;
More color every hour.
The news soon spread and hordes of folks
Are clogging up the roads
And tramping through our fields and yards.
We're trapped in our abodes.

The time is short for taking in
This awe inspiring sight.
Field workers pick unopened buds
From early mom to night.
In a few weeks when the show has closed.
And tourists have gone away.
We locals will be awakened
To a less exciting day.

The Invasion

The swallows have returned again
And brought some reinforcements.
A sea of birds attacking me
With streams of mud in torrents.

Their little nests are made with love
And glued fast to survive.
With broom I try to dissuade one
Before some more arrive.

They're building everywhere they see
A niche on which to hitch
Along the porch upon the eaves,
To them I am a witch

Because I won't allow them
To build homes above my door.
They bring their straw and glue it down,
I tear it down once more.

I must be ever vigilant
Before their nests are filled.
I'm not the fiend they think I am,
No hatchlings will be killed.

We have this squabble every spring,
A row I dare not lose,
Or I'll be trapped by their intent
To build where ere they choose.

Forgive me please, I've no more time
To sit and play with words.
I must take up my broom and wage
"The Battle of The Birds".

The Spring That Never Was

Our spring is leaving quietly
Before it truly came.
A day of sun just now and then
Is truly not the same

As the lovely spring we dreamed about
In winter's too long stay.
In a short time, spring will be gone
On another rainy day.

The berries are not ripening
And fields were seeded late.
Nature is calling all the shots
To seal a farmer's fate.

We weep for all the others
Who have suffered more than we.
The quakes, the floods and tornados
Have brought such misery.

We must reach out to one and all
And share each other's pain,
Knowing that some day, some year,
The sun will shine again.

The Blackberry and the Rose

The wild blackberry villain
Fell in love with my sweet rose.
I found them in the garden
All entangled in love's throes.

I took the hoe and hit him hard
With all the strength I had.
How could my hybrid beauty
Be seduced by such a cad?

I only meant to whack him down;
The sun got in my eyes.
My darling, little blossom
Met an early, sad demise.

Now my rose lies motionless
Betrayed by her wanton way;
Deserted by her false lover,
Who led her far astray.

I know that coward's hiding
Beneath the sheltering ground.
Hiding, plotting, planning, scheming,
Another to take down.

Dear one, turn away that fraud
Don't believe his selfish boast.
He will take you to his level,
Then thrive on your compost.

It is true that we are known
By the company we keep.
Hobnobbing with a scoundrel
Brings a price that mighty steep.

Spring Awakens

This morning I awakened to the light;
The bright day that you had prepared for me.
I thank you for your angel in the night
Who guarded me in sleep so carefully.

Please let me use this day that you have given
In works that will be pleasing unto you.
Let no one on this Earth or in your Heaven
Hear phrases from my lips that are untrue.

The hills I gaze on through my window pane
Are covered with the winter's fallen snow.
They tower over the expectant plain
And watch as Spring brings forth her early show.

The pine trees shaking off their snowy cover,
Deciduous trees with leaves in shades of green,
And I, excited as an eager lover
Watch as exploding blooms complete the scene.

These are but the first actors in the drama
And many more are waiting in the wings.
With gratitude I view the panorama
And marvel at the glory springtime brings.

I thank you Lord for giving me this season,
When all my world is fresh, lovely and new.
May I be worth this beauty beyond reason
And play my part in thankfulness to you.

Peaceful Moments

I sit on my stoop and survey my domain,
Can't think of a reason I have to complain.
The fuchsia is thirsty, I give it a squirt
And some for the dahlia, it truly can't hurt.

My roses are blooming, the birds are about
Teaching their nestlings to sing, there's no doubt.
It's the first days of summer and bees are abuzz
Working as hard as a busy bee does.

Though I know my Utopia won't be for long
And sooner or later some thing will go wrong
For this peaceful moment, all's right in my world
As my nation's flag flies, unfettered, unfurled.

For two-hundred thirty-three years she has flown
These bits of bright color that Betsy has sewn.
We'll all be saluting her on her birthday,
Old soldiers will march and the school bands will play.

We'll think of those who have so bravely gone
To fight for our flag so that we can go on
With such peaceful moments of sweetness and light
As we pray for their safety and end of their fight.

Poet's Delight

Sweet narcissus recurvus,
The poet's daffodil,
She's been around five-hundred years,
Perhaps she always will.

Not Wordsworth's common yellow,
Petals of pristine white
And fragrance unforgettable
A poeticus delight.

Graceful petals curling back
Revealing scented cup.
Bright butterflies warmed by the sun
Will stop awhile to sup.

With lavish hand I've planted her
To fill my yard en masse
With such ethereal beauty that
The brighter blooms are crass.

I cannot wait for bonny May
When first her charms appear,
Reminding me as sure as Spring,
She will return each year.

Facts of Life

I saw an eagle, hawk and heron
As I drove to town today.
Each sat in calm aloofness
With a watchful eye for prey.

I'm glad I'm not a bunny,
A small bird or a mouse.
For with such predators about,
I'd dare not leave my house

If I were a frog or fish I would
Sit still with eyes closed tight
Knowing that big heron could
Devour me with one bite.

My Lord gave me dominion
Over land and beast and fowl
And made me big enough I can't
Be picked off by an owl.

I find living to be tolerable,
Quite peaceful and serene,
But many smaller beings know
That nature can be mean.

So next time I feel like crying
And grumbling at my fate
I'll remember all those creatures
Who would think my life is great.

"Survival of the Fittest" is
The rule by which they live.
Dying is the price of living
They accept it and forgive.

Flat Stanley Visits the Skagit Valley

Flat Stanley needed some time off
to have a little fun.
Cassidie thought her grandpa
would be the very one
to show him the sights and glories of
a great metropolis;
so she sent him off to Seattle
with a farewell wave and kiss.

Now I don't know all that Grandpa did
to show him a good time, but
Stanley came to see me too;
the reason for this rhyme.
April in our valley is
a true sight to behold,
with fields of flaming tulips
and daffodils of gold.

When first he came, I fed him.
He looked so strangely flat.
If Grandpa gave him food to eat
I don't know where it's at.
Then I told him that I'd take him for
a long floriferous stroll.
I knew those fields of flowers would
be food for Stanley's soul.

When Stanley saw those lovely flowers
all he could do was smile.
I took him from my pocket
and let him run awhile.
He smelled of the pretty tulips
and laughed with pure elation;
he was so glad to see them
on his Washington vacation.

I live in Northern Washington
in the wonderful Puget Sound,
in the lovely Skagit Valley,
the most beautiful place around.
I'm Cassidie's great grandaunt Joyce
and I'd like for her to know
that I want her to come with him
if Flat Stanley wants to go

On another trip to these parts
when he gets some itching feet.
Like he, she'd think this country is
extremely hard to beat.

Delayed Spring

We're still waiting for true springtime
Though the flowers do not care.
They raise sweet, adoring faces
To the sun that isn't there.

The apple blossoms flutter down
Like snow flakes not long gone.
Housekeeping wind comes whirling in
To send them twirling on.

The weatherman has promised
Warmer weather coming soon,
But Spring won't have much time to stay
If Summer comes in June.

The Blackberry and the Rose

The wild blackberry villain
Fell in love with my sweet rose.
I found them in the garden
All entangled in love's throes.

I took the hoe and hit him hard
With all the strength I had.
How could my hybrid beauty
Be seduced by such a cad?

I only meant to whack him down;
The sun got in my eyes.
My darling, little blossom
Met an early, sad demise.

Now my rose lies motionless
Betrayed by her wanton way;
Deserted by her false lover,
Who led her far astray.

I know that coward's hiding
Beneath the sheltering ground.
Hiding, plotting, planning, scheming,
Another to take down.

Dear one, turn away that fraud
Don't believe his selfish boast.
He will take you to his level,
Then thrive on your compost.

It is true that we are known
By the company we keep.
Hobnobbing with a scoundrel
Brings a price that mighty steep.

The White Owl

The white or snowy owl is regal
And much larger than most owls.
And surely he is more beautiful
Than many ordinary fowls.

His home is in the far, far, north
But in the winter time
He can be spotted in the forty-eight
And thus this little rhyme.

My husband was excited
A year or so ago or more,
When he spotted and owl he hadn't seen
In our area before.

We looked owls up on the Internet
And were surprised to see
A picture of a snowy owl
Who looked the same as he.

We extended him a welcome
And hoped he'd want to stay
But alas! The time he spent with us
Was just a single day.

The Cascades

Mount Baker, seen from my window,
Is framed in his blanket of snow
towering over his neighbors, and
Admired from the valley below.
His beauty can't be disputed,
the poets and artists concur.
His jealous sister is angry . . .
He's taking attention from her.

She's proud of the fact she is taller,
than all of her brothers save one,
resenting Rainier for his stature,
he's too near her loved god, the sun.
Mount Hood, Mount Adams and others,
who make up the great Cascade Range,
have at one time or other, ignored her.
She vows this contempt shall soon change.

St. Helens could hold it no longer.
Her deep-seated smoldering rage.
She vents it early one morning,
The anger she'd held for an age.
The havoc she wrought is immense.
She feels no regret and no shame.
She's striking a blow for sisterhood.
The world will remember her name.

She forfeits some of her beauty,
Which passing of time will reclaim.
Her brothers now bow to her fury.
She basks in her ill gotten fame.
These mountains are slumbering giants.
Their power is yet to be seen.
They're holding their strength in abeyance;
Giving Helens her reign as queen.

We love our mountains, unheeding the danger,
we daringly dwell at their feet,
knowing full well, we're under the spell
of idols with dues swift and steep.
St. Helens has sounded a warning
with some of us paying the price.
We stay though aware of the perils,
encased in that beautiful ice.

Resurrection

Little brown orb,
lying so softly in my hand;
the marvel of you demanding my attention.
Could I but see deep into your heart,
I'd find a perfectly formed flower
waiting there.

Waiting for me,
to stir the rich brown earth and make a bed,
a room to hold you through the winter storms.
What life force induces you to grow
and not decay in your dark tomb?
Who guides you?

Lovingly
I cradle you and croon a lullaby.
Fragile skin splits and bares your creamy flesh.
Seemingly much too delicate to survive the
frosts and heaves to come.
I place you there.

Sleep little one.
In hibernation let the good earth nourish you.
Your internal clock, set by Nature,
will waken you to spring;
triumphantly breaking free,
a lovely tulip blossom.

September Rewards

Is there anything more splendid
Than a garden in the fall?
When your work is almost ended
And it's time to reap it all.

The great bounty's beyond endless
All you need and so much more.
It is offered with such largesse;
Some to eat and much to store.

The old pear tree is so loaded,
"Twill be hard to pick it all.
Is there anything so lovely
As a pear tree in the fall?

The apple tree won't be outdone;
She's Madam Beneficence,
The plum and nut trees firmly vie
For first in magnificence.

Oh a garden in the springtime
Is a place of hope and cheer.
But a garden isn't perfect
Until fall, at last, is here.

I remember Daddy bringing
All the produce, with a grin.
And my mama bravely canning
The profusion he brought in.

The cellar is overloaded.
And the bright jars line the wall.
Nothing is so satisfying
As the harvest in the fall.

The Turnover

I feel a hint of fall today,
Soon summer will be on her way.
It's time for mild and shorter days,
Sometimes seen through a smoky haze.

Smoke comes from forest fires afar
That will for long years leave a scar
On pristine beauty of this land,
Caused by small spark the wind had fanned.

There'll be no bum of leaves this year,
It has been dry and fires we fear.
Now with leaf burning out of style,
We'll put them on the compost pile.

We'll miss the bonfires and the fun
But better to be safely done.
Next spring we'll spread the compost and
Bring beauty back to barren land.

Storms Foretold

This storm brings back the former years
When my dear Daddy's brain and brawn
Were all we had to rely on.
No TV weatherman to tell
The depth of snow before it fell.
With Dad on watch we had no fears.
He seemed to know without TV
How long the winter storm would be.
Our pantry was pre-filled with food.
The big box over-flowed with wood.
No storm could catch him unprepared.
He saw with his wise weather eye
If clouds would stay or roll on by.
And when a blizzard he deemed due,
He'd say, "No school today for you."
Thus from the danger we were spared.
No weatherman today can know
As much as Daddy did of snow.

Winter Rains

You know me very well and that
 I'm not one to complain.
But dear Lord in the wintertime,
I get so tired of rain.

I wouldn't want to have Your job
With everyone to please.
Could you save some for our summer
When we have droughts to ease?

I took a turn about my yard
To check my winter garden.
The plants have all been watered well
And my impudence please pardon.

I'd like a little sunshine please,
To boost my sagging spirit.
A bit of warmth to sooth my soul
If such reward I merit.

But if You have a larger plan,
Intend more clouds to bring;
I'll put my garden tools away
And wait awhile for Spring.

Rains of Winter

Rains of winter are often tiring
As well as relentlessly unending.
Our poet finds them uninspiring.
She regrets the hours she has been spending
On poetry, tiring and unending.

She tries to hit a lighter note
By turning to reading of the bards.
Comparing them to what she wrote
In a swift turning of the cards.
She wishes she wrote like the bards.

The reading brightens somber mood
And brings sunshine into the room.
Her own lines now, are looking good.
She has shaken off the clouds of gloom.
Gone, somber mood and veils of doom.

Wild Love

The blackberry's love for the garden rose,
Brought down the gardener's wrath.
The blackberry sensed the danger,
As he wended the garden path.

"A love so true as mine," he sighed,
"Must dare to brave the hoe,
Just a few more feet to reach her.
My true love she must know."

He crept along so quietly,
Sometimes quite out of sight.
Until he nudged his darling's feet.
Did he dare to trust the light?

He heard the gardener's heavy boot,
And hid in craven shame.
He knew he'd soon be weeded out,
A seedling with no name.

"Have I no worth since I don't rate
Some Latin nomenclature?
Without a well-known parentage,
Am I a freak of nature?"

His darling's line was long and pure.
No skeletons in her past.
He had to make his feelings known.
Those boots were treading fast.

Gently then he wrapped his vine
Around his loved one's spine.
In great amazement he opined,
"Her thorns are sharp as mine."

The sweet rose felt his tender touch,
And realized his fear,
And wondered at his bravery,
In coming to her here.

She heard the swishing of the hoe,
She heard those nearing feet.
Quietly letting down her leaves,
In a manner so discreet.

She covered her wild lover.
The gardener unaware.
Stopped but to view her beauty.
He saw naught hiding there.

She whispered "You are safe now."
The blackberry's heart was light.
Thankful that his dear sweet rose.
Had not exposed his plight.

"A rose is still a rose," she said,
"By any other name.
And in our distant ancestry,
We share some of the same."

" I'd rather know your wild love,
Than a lover dull and tame."
And cuddling close, gave back his kiss,
Without a bit of shame.

Next season, there were seedlings,
Of a very different kind.
The gardener delighted, cried,
"A horticultural find."

The moral of this story,
Things aren't always what they seem.
The one you look down on today.
Could be tomorrow's dream.

Dear Reader, weigh these stories well,
Learn not to judge too fast.
Be sure you have heard every view.
Before your vote is cast.

Winter Friends

The gathered birds are making
Such a cacophonous sound.
It is their way of telling me
They now are onward bound.

They are rounding up the young,
Reminding every single bird.
They are so loud I am quite sure
That every bird has heard.

The blackbirds, starlings, swallows,
Are headed on their way.
It's time to fill the feeders now
For the little ones that stay.

The chickadees and juncos,
The towhees and that bunch,
Will be pecking at my window,
And begging for their lunch.

For just a few small handouts,
They will keep me entertained
And chase away my doldrums,
When all I see is rain.

With unspoken agreement.
They'll provide the fun and song.
My part their food and water,
The whole cold winter long.

Spiritual

My World

In the middle of the Universe I stand,
In the wonder of a world prepared for me.
God provided all I need
With some cautions I should heed.
As well as ears to hear and eyes to see.
He filled it with variety of song
From lovely birds, returning every year.
And with grasses, flowers and trees
And a mild and warming breeze
That tells me spring is waiting to appear.
He sends no bill to pay at end of day
And no millionaire could buy what He gives free.
It is really only fair
That he asks me to take care
And no being goes extinct because of me.
We don't know if in this universe immense
There is another world as wonderful as ours
Where even the fertile sod
Is a gracious gift from God
Along with all the sunshine and rain showers.
Everything this world needs, our God has given
And the only realm more perfect is God's Heaven.

Jesus is the Answer

Jesus is the answer
when your world is dark and drear.
Jesus is the answer
when every-body here
on Earth is bringing you to grief.
Nowhere you turn brings you relief;
consumed are you with doubt and fear.
Remember what you learned
at your sainted mother's knee.
"Jesus is the answer
to all questions there may be."
Her words brought solace to you then;
they'll chase all doubt and worry when
repeating them with true belief,
 accepting Jesus as your Chief
in faith you are that child again.

Jesus is the answer
to the what, the where, the how.
Jesus is the answer;
you knew it then you know it now.

It is Finished

"It is finished," cried our Lord
As He died upon the tree
In magnificent obedience
To His Father's firm decree.

He knew well that he was going
Toward that lonely hillside cave
As He rode with "Alleluias"
Men's deceitful souls to save.

How His brave heart must have broken
As He traveled forth to die
When the cries of adulation turned
To shouts of "Crucify".

I'd like to think I would have stayed there
With the sad and faithful few
Who were with him through his ordeal
As the senseless anger grew.

I hope I would have brought him water
As He moaned with dreadful thirst
And would have stayed to hold His mother
To protect her from the worst.

And I hope that unlike Peter
I'd be too loyal to deny
That I knew my loving Savior
Who for me and you would die.

Heavy Chains

These heavy chains, so restraining
Have been forged by me and you.
We built them strong, no human hands
Can cut these chains in two.
We created them by living
In a wasteful, sinful way.
One link at a time, we forged them
As weights we wear today.

These irons will not be loosened
Until He turns the key
It matters not how we struggle.
They'll only tighter be.
If we turn to our dear Savior
And ask forgiveness now
He will happily undo them
Our freedom to endow.

We cannot know what it is like
To be completely free
Until God has forgiven us.
He waits for you and me.

When All I've Loved

When all whom I have loved are gone,
Dear Lord, when I'm the only one,
Who cares if I should live or die,
When there is no one left to cry;

Then Lord, take me.
But if there is a single soul
For whom I play important role,
Who might just stumble, lose his way
Without my guidance for a day,

Then I would be
Content to stay another while
To give him courage, bring a smile;
Teach him to look to You above,
For truest guidance, purest love,
His way to see.

Then I would say "My work is done.
On Earth there is no other one,
Who needs the love I have to give,
No reason now, for me to live."
Dear Lord, take me.

Unending Prayers

Dear Father, forgive me for grumbling,
"My request wasn't granted again."
I expectantly asked You for sunshine,
While another prayed harder for rain.

Please grant me the wisdom to notice
That the world doesn't turn around me.
You've answered my prayers in the best way
Only You the almighty can see.

So the next time I ask for a favor
Whether praying for rain or the sun,
I'll remember to end with self-effacing words, "
Not my will but Your big will be done."

Adam and Wife

God viewed the work that
he had done In six short days and it was good.
But there was no one there to see
The beauty and the magnitude.
He said I need to make a man
In my own image, one who will
Enjoy the wonders I have made.
Such beauty cannot help but thrill.

He took some dust and formed it and
Before Him the man Adam stood;.
Who gazed at all the beauty round
He looked and saw that it was good.
All of the beasties came in pairs,
But the first man was all alone.
God said, "I'll make a helpmeet too,
This garden shall be theirs to own."

He took a rib from Adam's side,
And fashioned Eve as big as life.
And Adam saw, said, "This is good."
As God pronounced them man and wife.
A wedding gift He gave to them.
The lovely garden free and clear
Permission too, to eat the fruit,
Except one tree they were to fear.

They were a disobedient pair,
And hadn't learned of gratitude.
They tasted the forbidden fruit,
Then ate some more for it was good.
They tried to hide their sin from God.
For not obeying as they should,
God drove them out into the world.
They looked and saw it wasn't good.

And that is how sin came to be.
All starting with that wicked pair.
Are we so sure that we might not
Have tasted too, had we been there?
They left the garden and they lost
The fellowship they had with God.
It is the same unto this day,
We choose the path that Adam trod.

But God has given us a chance
To change before our final days.
He sent His beloved son to die
And bring us from our sinful ways.
Much greater than the garden fair,
Our gift of life if we believe.
We call upon dear Jesus' name.
And God's forgiveness we'll receive.

The Garden still awaits us there,
If we are living as we should.
When welcomed to that Holy Place.
We'll look and know that it is good.

His Messenger

When all my days have faded
Into someone else's memory
Will they recall I loved the Lord
And tried his messenger to be?

Will they remember words I said
To guide them safely on their way?
Please give me words of wisdom, Lord
That will survive beyond my day.

Words that may clear the troubled path
For loved one's coming after me;
Reminding them to look to You
Their ever faithful Guide to be.

Here Outside of Eden

Here outside of Eden
I'm lost and prone to roam.
The earth is beautiful it's true,
But it is not my home.
For I remember Eden
So glorious it seems
Its beauty comes to haunt me
And tease me in my dreams.

God created Eden
And offered man the best
Of all its fruits and glories.
If he could pass the test.
By yielding to temptation
Man committed the first sin
And here outside of Eden
He yearns to get back in.

Faith

Faith is a powerful thing
As true believers can aver
I learned this at my mother's knee.
The lessons learned from her
Have stayed with me for life
In good times and in bad.

Some time I've strayed away
And faith of Mom and Dad
Protected me from this world's wiles.
On other days remembering
Wonder of their love and smiles
Enabled me to find way through
Rueful, and sometimes lonely miles.

Forever grateful I unbeaten by my woes
Live on with certain faith.
That my faithful God is close.
He guides and guards me every day
In sunshine or in rain
No matter if I fall
God is there to ease my pain.

The Day of Rest

Do you recall from long ago,
The special feel of Sunday?
When all of time was set on slow,
And work was left for Monday?

Of course we had to milk the cow.
Daddy allowed that was all right.
But hand must never touch the plow.
On the Sabbath, day or night.

Sunday school began at ten.
Then came the preacher's sermon
Sometimes he talked too long and then,
It would be hard to keep from squirming.

Daddy said "Amen" out loud.
Some souls were ripe for reaping.
I sneaked a peek around the crowd,
To see who might be sleeping.

I tried to keep my pious thought,
 Didn't want to be a sinner.
This silent searching only brought,
Eagerness for Sunday dinner.

Mother ready if she could,
So she needn't work on Sunday.
But fixing good meals for her brood,
No putting off 'til Monday.

Dressing chickens the day before,
All ready for the skillet.
She could clean a pullet for herself,
But Daddy had to kill it.

Biscuits light enough to fly.
Mashed potatoes and gravy too.
And then perhaps her apple pie
Were on Mother's Sunday menu.

The preacher used to come around,
Perhaps he could smell her cooking.
He'd take an extra piece of pie,
And hope God wasn't looking.

The rest of that long afternoon,
Was reserved for having fun day.
But Daddy said "Don't be too loud.
Remember it is Sunday."

Those peaceful days are in the past.
For now its malls and shopping,
Or motor cars or baseball games,
And even some bar hopping.

I would that time could take me back.,
To those Sunday days of rest.
To Mother's meals and quiet time,
And a day God truly blessed.

Alone With God

For five long days I've been snowbound
My home with blanket pulled around
Is quiet as the distant hill
That nestles in its white surround.

My world so very still.
No small birds trill to break the spell,
All vanished with the flakes that fell.
Electric voice immobilized,

Marooned in solitary cell,
My world strangely disguised.
No noisome birdsong to intrude
On absolute of quietude.

No foot on yielding snow has trod.
Suspended in rare interlude,
Alone, alone with God.
The snow remover coming through,

The telephone and power crew;
Although their efforts I applaud,
I miss the peaceful time I knew
Alone, alone with God.

Accompanied

Thank you Lord for walking with me
Through the shadowed vales and valleys,
Holding when I blindly stumble
'Til my flagging spirit rallies.
When you take the larger burden
Relieving me of its great heft;
You ask only that I carry
The modest portion that is left

I was feeling sad and lonely
On that dark journey all alone;
Forgetting you were there with me.
I was not ever on my own.
Now that I've survived the danger
And I have safely swum to shore,
I know big waves would have swamped me
Had you not carried me once more.

Miscellaneous

Changing Fashions

The piercing of their body parts
In the precocious young
Makes me shudder with revulsion
But I try to hold my tongue.

I remember how my daddy,
When I dared to cut my hair,
Vowed his sisters wouldn't do that
And I said I didn't care.

I just thought he was old fashioned
Stuck back in another age.
Did he know this was the forties
And we'd turned another page?

He didn't know why any woman
Wanted to paint up her face.
Wearing lipstick and eye makeup
Was a scandalous disgrace.

Now I see that I'm becoming
More like Daddy every day.
Simply shocked at how the young folks
Put their bodies on display.

I resent studs in their noses
In their navels and their brows.,
But I smile and keep my quiet.
I know better than to grouse.

I smile, knowing a small secret,
The time will come they'll have to pay.
When their kids become more daring
Than they are themselves today.

Or it may be we've reached the limit;
There just might be a turn around.
Old standards will be new again,
Just waiting to be found.

Broken Promise

When the girls with whom you've flirted
All have gone their merry way,
Winning hearts, dispensing favors
In the flavor of the day

There is one whose kept the home fires,
While her lonely heart has yearned.
Will she still be there to hold you
After your last bridge is burned?

Weigh temptation, is it worth it,
Seeking love for just the day?
Will there still be one who needs you
When all others go away?

When a loving heart is broken,
It won't be an easy mend.
Your promised heart to her forever,
Is no longer yours to lend.

If tomorrow, God should call you,
Take you from the life he gave,
Only she will long remember
To put flowers on your grave.

Hurry home now, Casanova,
Heed my warning and beware.
If too late you seek the home fires,
It may be she won't be there.

Paul Bunyan

Hardly a man is now alive
Who remembers Minnesota
Before Paul Bunyan flattened it
To match with North Dakota.

His blue ox Babe was equal to
Most any thing he'd ask.
A job that takes machines today,
Babe found an easy task.

When Minnesota was cleared off
To Paul's high satisfaction,
He looked around for more to do.
His huge ox needed action.

He came out to the great Northwest
Where he found to his surprise,
The trees grew taller and so big
They matched his ox for size.

Babe struggled just to clear a path
For wagons to get through.
Paul, fearing for his valiant ox
Said, "I'm retiring you."

As I said before, no man's alive
To tell the end of story.
It's said Paul and his ox went home
To bask in their past glory.

A Multitude of Pies

In harvest time in grateful awe,
We picked all the fruit we saw,
To bake into delicious pies.
Each crust hides holiday surprise.

We've already frozen all the berries,
And in July we gathered cherries.
Now pears and plums and apples wait
Our appetites for pies to sate.

And my own favorite, oh my,
Is anything better than peach pie?
Our garden too, has given forth
Pumpkins for many a pie's worth.

Tempting to every Bill or Phil
As they cool on my window sill.
With crust that crumbles in one's mouth,
Birds wait for taste before flying South.

My grandchildren come in every size
And each one wants his favorite pies.
For Christmas I've favored ones for each,
And for myself, I keep the peach.

Flood Warning

The river is rising
There's no time to lose.
Gather the valuables
What do I choose?
Shall I run ? Shall I stay?
Will it flood? Go away?
There's no one to help me decide.
I'm in danger, with no place to hide.

My neighbor just stopped,
He says I should leave.
I know that I ought,
But it's hard to believe.
Wish I lived in a tower
There'd be no need to worry.
I'll just shut off the power,
Is it coming? Best hurry!

My good dog and I'll run away,
To find a high place we can stay.

Glowing Fairies

I wonder if the fireflies glow
As they did in the long ago
In summer evenings on the prairies.
I'd chase them, saying they were fairies.

I never caught a firefly
They were not there, I don't know why,
When I had clutched them in my hand
And I could never understand
Where they had gone, those flashing fairies
So long ago on virgin prairies.

It's been so many years since I
Have seen any of them flitting by.
Perhaps fairy queens and fireflies
Don't show their selves to aged eyes.

Fairy Facts

Fairies too get thirsty
And one just might come to sup
And linger for a moment at
Inviting nectar cup.

If it happens you should see her
Do not take the time to blink
For a fairy though she's tiny
Is much faster than you think.

She resembles a small hummer
As she dips and darts on high
Or perhaps you could mistake her for
A lovely butterfly.

If you think your eyes deceive you
Then a secret I will tell
You must listen for the tinkle of
Her minute fairy bell.

If you should hear and see her
 Do not dare to look away
For fantastic, friendly fairies
Do not visit every day.

First Car

"Look Ma, I'm driving."
His eyes sparkle with the thrill.
Mama sees the teenager
And not her little Will.

Too soon the time will come when he
Asks for the real car keys.
"Don't let him grow too fast, Lord.
Just keep him little, please."

She knows she can't be there each time
His hand is on the throttle.
Thankful that day has not yet come.
She goes to fetch his bottle.

Familiar Love

Familiar love, like ticking clock,
Kept every day sound filled.
Its steadiness unheard by me
Until the voice was stilled.

The TV turned to football game;
A softly clearing throat,
Merely background noises
Of which to take no note.

The sound of running water in
Routine daily showers,
So tranquil, but in memory,
So loud it overpowers.

Soft rustling of the paper
As he turned another page;
His noise of indignation
When he read of some outrage.

The quiet in this winter
Of my life is hard to bear.
How can one miss the constancy,
Unnoticed when it's there?

So loud, the ticking of the clock.
On my cheek a silent tear.
In homage to those little sounds,
No longer there to hear.

Dressed in Style

Though some were shocked
inclined to scold,
"The dress you wear
is much to bold."
My Grandma smiled
and calmly said,
"Your granddad liked me
dressed in red."

"This is the day
we honor him.
Forgive me if
I scorn the prim
and proper way
my age should dress.
Though you may not
agree, I guess.
I like the way
It makes me feel
As my true colors
I reveal."

"Today I wear
this scarlet hue
for him and self
and not for you."

Country School

You can see the children coming
Down the winding country lanes
To the little prairie schoolhouse
On the North Dakota plains.

Some of them are riding horses,
Others walk a mile or so.
While some come to school by auto
If Dad has one that will go.

You will see no yellow busses
Buzzing 'round the countryside.
A ride to school for learning
All the parents must provide.

At noon, you'll find the big boys
Playing baseball in the spring,
Or catching prairie gophers
With a length of twine or string.

The sophisticated older girls
Sit still and talk of boys
While the younger children scramble
For the school yard's few big toys.

There is one lopsided go a round,
Some dilapidated slides.
But the coveted amusement
Is a set of giant strides.

The big boys have discovered
They can wrap one giant stride
Around the others and one boy
Will have a thrilling ride.

There is danger in that play yard,
Lucky none of them are dead.
As they ride a loose slide often
Will hit someone on the head.

The school bell rings at nine am
Fifteen minutes liberate
An hour for lunch, another break,
At four emancipate.

I am speaking of the way it was
When I was in that school
Where but one teacher taught us
And we learned the golden rule.

Those school houses have disappeared;
Torn down or hauled away.
The children are great- grandparents
In this more progressive day.

It now takes a pile of teachers
To fill up one youngster's head.
And to catch a bus at seven
Children stumble out of bed.

They will miss the hearty breakfasts
That their own grand-parents ate.
If they are not there to catch it
That yellow school bus will not wait.

Oh I'm sure that things are better now.
But back then we learned to spell
In a little country school-house
And survived, the tale to tell.

Last Night I Dreamed

Last night I dreamed of youthful days,
when all the world was new.
The faces of the long ago
were there for me to view.
Old friends appeared to me again,
we chatted for awhile,
I recognized their voices,
their laughter and each smile.

And he was there, my first love
with his beloved touch.
He hadn't changed, I felt the same
as when we loved so much.
This morning I awakened
to a pillow wet with tears.
I've been taking flowers to his grave
for over forty years.

Some, whom I had dreamed about,
had left without a trace.
The others had gone on before
their judgment call to face.
Why did I dream about them?
Why were they sent to me?
Did they each bring me a message,
something I need to see?

Perhaps God sent them as a gift
to show that they still care,
that when it's time to join them
I will find a welcome there.

Lost Dreams

Your Grandma's feeling sad today.
You may have seen her cry.
Someone is gone forever,
Whom she'd hoped would never die.

She's remembering the long ago
When she was just a girl
And his piercing blue eyes from the screen
Could set her heart awhirl.

He is gone with all the others
Who had played important part
In her dreams and silly fancies
Before Grandpa had her heart.

Richard and Kirk and Gregory
Burt and Rock, Jimmy and John.
Henry and Frank and Montgomery,
All of her idols gone.

Each had taken a little piece
Of a sweet and carefree time
When these heroes of the magic screen
Were hers for just a dime.

She's crying for Joanne and Paul
And just a little for herself.
As she buys the salad dressing
Bearing his face, on the shelf.

I Remember

When neighbors came to visit
And we'd just sit for awhile
Mama would cut her new baked cake
And serve it with a smile.

Or perhaps we'd have a game of cards
Of Rummy, maybe Whist
We'd talk about the folks passed on
And how much they were missed.

The new preacher might be discussed.
Some called him high-faluty.
Until Mama reminded quietly,
"To save us is his duty."

Those days are gone and now we sit
In front of our big TV.
We learn about the whole wide world
And our neighbors never see.

I Remember

until time takes me
into Never-Never Land
I shall remember

the one of a kind,
delicious as a thumb print cookie
dimple in your chin.

shared ice-cream sodas
two sets of brown eyes gazing
melting with each bite

green grasses cover
your long years ago dug grave
I still remember

My Encounter With the Famous

"Mr. Washington", I asked him,
"How do you think we've done
With the country that you left us,
When your worthy race was run"?
"I'm amazed," he said, "at progress
In two hundred years and plus
In ways not the same country
You inherited from us.
I'm proud you've tried so hard to keep
The Constitution strong
And years have proven us to have been
More often right than wrong.
I sighed and said, "We've failed some times".
He answered, "That is true,
But you have picked up the pieces
And kept on battling through.
If brave men don the mantle
And hold their standards high,
Then we signers will in all truth say,
"It was worth the do or die".

Little A1 Writing a Roundelay

Little A1 writing a roundelay
Worked on his poetry all day;
While brother John with resounding whoop
Skipped along with a stick and hoop.
Each was happy in his own way.

John wondered why A1 would not come play
But who was happier would you say;
John running and playing loop the loop
Or little A1 writing a roundelay?

Next morning the sky was dark and gray.
The storm clouds would not go away.
John settled on the backdoor stoop
With a big bowl of Mother's soup.
He was pleased to sit with a luncheon tray
While little A1 wrote his roundelay.

Letting Go

Little boy with hair in curl,
Pretty as most any girl.
Feed you well to make you grow
Wishing time would go more slow.

Watching with attentive eye
Guarding from the tricks you try.
Climbing in the apple tree.
Falling, may you fall on me.

Proud I am to see you growing,
Even though it's with the knowing
Each step is one more step away
From the little boy I love today.

For just this while I hold you tight,
Tuck you in to sleep at night,
Playing my part in bigger plan
For the little boy too soon a man.

Lost words

Sometimes I catch them,
The words I'm reaching for;
At other times watch helplessly
As they crash to the floor.
I try to reassemble but
They've landed in a jumble.
I grab too fast for floaters and
My chair and I both tumble.

Susie thinks it is hilarious
And joins into the fun.
Before she hears my "stop"
She has already swallowed one..
I am truly very sorry
There are no poems from me.
You will know why when I tell you
My dog ate my poetry.

Overkill

I was born before
drugs were for fun,
brain's not been fried
'til overdone.
Of alcohol I take no taste.
A mind's too valuable
to waste.

Then why do thoughts
begin to scramble
and memories often
fade or ramble?
Have the years brought on
this over-spill
and a brand new thought
is over-kill?

A few short steps from
the dreaded "A"?
It's best I write
my poem today!

Our Country as it Was Before

I believe in this U.S.A. that was before;
Before terrorists had come to our shore,
Before atom bombs and tumbling towers,
Before pollution and acid rain showers.

I believe in guilt free childhood days,
When our parents led us on life's pathways.;
When we loved neighbors and neighbors loved us
With our country at peace, no one made a fuss.

Was it all so peaceful as I recall?
When Mother hovered and kept my world small?
I long to go back to those days so bright,
When my beloved country was good and right.

Not Allowed

My granddaughters get to do things,
Their grandma never could.
Good girls didn't do those things,
But sort a wished they could.
I always was a good girl
And made my mama proud,
But there were just too many things
That simply weren't allowed.
My papa never kissed Mama
'Til they were proper wed;
For good girls didn't act that way
Is what my mama said..
I had not a single choice of
Being anything but good.
If my parents hadn't caught me
My four big brothers would.
For Mama's sake I always was
As good as I could be;
Except perhaps the time that I;
Well, you won't hear that from me.
So dear Granddaughters be good girls
And make your grandma proud.
And thank your lucky stars that now
More things are quite allowed.

Nightfall (A villanelle)

The night has come and I have lost my way.
With recklessness, I frittered daylight hours.
Surprised am I at ending of the day.

Refusing guidance, I began to stray,
Paid no attention to the threat of showers.
The night has come and I have lost my way.

Confused as whether it is wise to stay,
I tremble at the sight of hovering towers.
Surprised am I at ending of the day.

Dark clouds have covered the full moon's bright ray
And just ahead a menacing form cowers.
The night has come and I have lost my way.

Deep weariness has caused me great dismay.
I lie down in a bed of sweet wild flowers.
Surprised am I at ending of the day.

My guardian angel urges me to pray.
My safety is beyond my mortal powers.
The night has come and I have lost my way.
Surprised am I at ending of the day.

Not For Losers

You've joined the quite exclusive club
"The Over 90 Bunch."
If duty calls we answer with
"Denied. We're out to lunch."

We've worked hard and we've paid our dues
In summer, spring and fall.
And since we live on borrowed time.
It's precious after all.

The winter of our lives is ours
To do with as we please.
We've taught you well, now do the job
So we can take our ease.

If you should see some older folks
With a glass of wine or punch,
Who look like they are having fun,
We're the "Over Ninety Bunch."

Our Loved Flag

The flag of our nation flies so free and strong,
That star spangled banner of patriot song.
She's carried in honor, our red, white and blue
All over the earth, liberty to pursue.

Her presence means freedom to all of the world
On the tallest of mountains, our flag's been unfurled.
She's been planted firmly on the crust of the moon,
In Valley Forge snow and on Iraq's sand dune.

The fifty states joined in harmonious band
Combined in one union, our glorious land.
Each star of the flag representing a state
Each one to the other no more nor less great.

Our fathers and sons and our daughters have fought
That our flag to dishonor shall never be brought.
We salute it, we love it, we carry it high;
Tip your hat, touch your heart, our loved flag's passing by.

Who Cares?

I have reached the age of privilege
And I like it here a lot.
If I don't do what I oughta
I can say, "I plumb forgot."

If seven AM is too early,
I can stay awhile in bed.
Don't need to do what I don't want to,
Can do what I want instead.

Being younger wasn't always
What it was cracked up to be,
Not so great as I remember,
It's just my bad memory.

I don't worry about birthdays
Since they roll around so fast
The only reason now to note them
An excuse to have a blast.

Nothing much can happen to me
That I haven't faced before,
So I welcome the tomorrows
And adventures yet in store.

The Twilight

The time of day to power a poet's fancy
Are those short moments between day and night
When rosy glows streak in the west horizon;
That lovely interlude we call twilight.

Somewhere between the daylight and the darkness,
The remnants of the sun still hanging there
Erasing heavy burdens of the daytime;
Removing all the weariness and care.

The mystic time the poets call the gloaming,
This lingering salute to end of day,
Just long enough to usher in the nightfall
And welcome in the moon and stars display.

This half-light often brings quixotic dreaming
Even lulling birds and beasts to quietude;
This respite is God's gift for lonely spirits,
Bestowed on them to bless their solitude.

The Only Peach

I ate my peach today, the one that didn't fall.
The heavy rain and wind brought down the rest.
The slugs, the wasps and creatures got them all.

My son had lovingly planted my peach tree,
Before God called and took him far away.
Did he hold tight to this last fruit for me?

Last year there was a harvest I could share;
A young tree that had tried its very best.
This season all that bounty wasn't there.

I savored that peach as I knew I would,
Sweetened and covered with the richest cream.
When there's no more the taste is twice as good.

Now there's nothing left to do but wait a year,
Put up my feet, sit by the fire and dream;
Awaiting "Fruits of God" to reappear.

Seattle at Seafair Time

Each summer brings festivity
To the Emerald City by the sea
And Torchlight Parade in diversity
Of folks who live in harmony.

The people line the streets and cheer
As the Chinese dragons writhe and rear
Their heads from which come flaming fire.
While dancers prance in bright attire.
Then comes the dancing Vietnamese.
Are any more richly adorned than these?

The Koreans and the Filipinos
Come by in their flamboyant clothes
And all the while the floats arrive,
Each one that follows more contrived.
A streamered car holds Miss Seafair
As pretty girls wave back and stare
And each one dares to hope that she
Next year the Seafair Queen will be.

Children laugh and parents cheer
As clowns and pirates now appear
Tossing candy and t shirts too
Just as the whole long year they do
Visiting hospitals and other places,
Bringing smiles to sweet, sad, faces.

The parade on wide Fourth Avenue
Ends, but each day there's something new
To fill the days with joy and fun.
The Blue Angels will perform for one
Anticipated thrill and then
The boat races will begin.

Have you ever seen a hydroplane
In a race at speeds that are insane?
The month is one long barbecue
With exotic food cooked just for you.
In July and August, the place to be
Is the Emerald city by the sea.

The School-bus Driver's Prayer

Their parents and the school board
Trust me with this precious load.
May I never lose attention
As I drive on street or road.
Some will be new students, Lord.
Might I help to calm their fears?
Please fill my heart with love for them
As I wipe away their tears.

With my foot on the gas pedal
And Yours upon the brake,
We will do the job together,
Never making a mistake.
Another school-bus driver
Transports one I call my own.
May she turn to You each day, Lord
Knowing she is not alone.

They're the future of our nation
And their parent's pride and joy.
I remember this each morning
As I load a girl or boy.
A youngster may be unruly,
Disrespectful, even wild.
Help me to keep my patience, Lord.
He is someone's well loved child.

Prayer of a Lazy Gardener

Dear Lord, I love this season best.
My little garden is at rest.
You've sent your fresh, life giving rain,
Hydrating the parched Earth again.
I see once more I am too late,
Those greedy birds just would not wait.
Grapes not yet sweet enough for me,
They've eaten in their gluttony.
They had to stuff themselves I know
For the southward way they have to go.
Improvident laggard that I am,
I'm happy not to make that jam.

I've planted, harvested and stored
And leisure now is my reward.
I thank you for this time of rest
When I love gardening the best.
Seed catalogues I can peruse
And perhaps even take a snooze,
As I sit snugly by the fire
Dreaming the garden I desire.

Plea of the Prairie Wife

As a good mate she had followed
As he vowed to tame the West.
Though her life had not been easy,
She had done her very best.

Though the loneliness was endless
When he found the nomad life
Of a cattle trailing cowboy,
She was still his patient wife.

Far from genteel East and doctors,
She had just ignored the pain.
He found this note beside her
When he came back home again.

Lay me not in mausoleum
Entombed in an airless cave.
Bury me upon the prairie
Let a field stone mark my grave.

I was never much for grandeur,
Simple ginghams mine to wear.
Dress me not in silks and satins
Just to see me lying there.

Bury me upon the prairie.
It has been my beloved home.
Bury me among the wildflowers
Where so often I would roam.

Until wakened for the judgment
By the trumpets up above,
Let me lie in sweet surrender
To the prairie that I love.

Playing the Game

When God put us down on this chessboard called life,
He didn't issue a password to keep us from strife.
The price that we pay for the freedom of will
Is the fact that we know there is no magic pill
Protecting us from the results of our moves.
God's a fan in the stands for the children he loves.
Before we started playing, he gave us the tools
To make us winners if we follow the rules.
God is no puppeteer, pulling the string.
It is all up to us to make our lives sing.
God didn't invent the automobile
And he didn't put that fool at the wheel.
I do not believe that life's pre-ordained.
Then why would we try, there would be nothing gained.
Man is responsible for his own action.
So don't be like unto that self excuse faction
Who blame God when truly the fault is their own.
God taught them to play then left them alone.
Just play the game well, do the best that you can.
God will be referee for the actions of man.

Pedigree

He knew that life was not a joke
He wouldn't buy a pig in poke.
He'd been raised with integrity
To be the best that he could be.

Farm grown, he learned to check for line,
Though first appearances were fine.
Filly or calf must stand the test;
He wanted nothing but the best.

When he bought his first used car
I knew this lad was going far.
It was plain to see he understood
He must first look beneath the hood.

When it was time to seek a wife,
His most important choice in life,
As if knowing what he was about
He reached in blindly, pulled one out.

In the game of sweet romance
A meddling mother has no chance,
Helpless in disbelief as he
Forgets to check her pedigree.

Young women don't be cross with me
You know it's true as it can be
You never buy inferior brand
No wonder I can't understand

That when its time to choose a mate,
You'd rather leave it up to fate.
I truly think it is a pity,
You choose him just because he's pretty.

Peaceful Moments

I sit on my stoop and survey my domain,
Can't think of a reason I have to complain.
The fuchsia is thirsty, I give it a squirt
And some for the dahlia, it truly can't hurt.

My roses are blooming, the birds are about
Teaching their nestlings to sing, there's no doubt.
It's the first days of summer and bees are abuzz
Working as hard as a busy bee does.

Though I know my utopia won't be for long
 And sooner or later some thing will go wrong'
For this peaceful moment, all's right in my world
As my nation's flag flies, unfettered, unfurled.

For two-hundred thirty-three years she has flown
These bits of bright color that Betsy has sewn.
We'll all be saluting her on her birthday,
Old soldiers will march and the school bands will play.

We'll think of those who have so bravely gone
To fight for our flag so that we can go on
With such peaceful moments of sweetness and light
As we pray for their safety and end of their fight.

The Old and New
Maverick Free verse

My grandmother's velvet covered album
was not coveted by any of my siblings.
I pretended not to care so as not spark their interest,
but I was happy when it was scorned by others.
It is now in my possession and proudly
shown on my coffee table.
Unlabeled photos from the 1800's fill it.
I can only guess who might be whom.
I try to find resemblances to my siblings, or myself
and make up stories to fit the characters.
The real stories of their lives are lost to the past.
How sad that they did not have the cameras and
videos of the modern age, to record they're stories.

My pictures are memories tucked into a silver frame
or in between some pages glued as part of the past.
My daddy sitting proud and tall, Mama's hand upon his arm
Driving his young and lively team.
I wrote their names on the back for posterity.
Here is one of their first cars, just see my mama's smile.
As I've heard tell it was the one that broke down every mile
As the many babies came along, they added them one
by one into the family portrait, seven kids all told.
Through marriages and grand-kids,
everyone is shown with pride.
Now with my labeled names and
other bits of information they will
be real to the following generations.

That Kodak recorded lifetimes, before it up and died.
They'd be surprised if they could see the pictures of today.
We take them now with digital and email them away to all..
I've gathered old and new alike, to place upon my screen.
In color or in black and white, my family's story
shall be saved for all who care . . .
Won 4th place John's Maverick Free contest.

True Beauty

The youthful beauty of an unlined face,
Unsullied by the use that lies ahead,
Has still the freshness of an unused space.
A book to show its worth must have been read.
True fairness shows when beauty dwells within,
No need to fear effects of time's swift pace.
Though chance of fate can its bright radiance dim
And leave sad mark on that beloved face.
Beauty untried is beauty quite unearned;
Fair to behold with worthiness unproved.
The cherished face with lines of living burned
Will to true lover, surely be more loved.
The beauty not reflected in the glass
Remains when more apparent charms shall pass.

Unwelcome Guest

Time marched ahead relentlessly
While I was unaware.
I jogged around the comer and
Old age was waiting there.

I didn't want to meet with her
But had to be polite.
She said she'd like to stay with me
Perhaps just over night.

I let her come, "Oh woe is me"
She hasn't gone away.
She brought such heavy baggage that
I fear she's here to stay.

A satchel full of aches and pains.
A bag of moans and groans.
She is becoming so entrenched
I feel her in my bones.

She follows me around all day
And spoils my appetite.
If I escape to early bed
She awakens me at night.

Take my advice dear younger friends
Don't stop to tell her "Hi".
If you should catch a glimpse of her
Just keep on jogging by.

Undying Words

I saved love notes from callow youths
Who set my heart aflutter
Until I met the one who could
Turn that same heart to butter.

The valentines he sent to me
Throughout the happy years
Are wrapped in finest tissue now
Though spotted by my tears.

The loveliest of all came in
The year he left forever
A sweet memento of the ties
That cruel death can't sever.

Though many lonely years have passed,
Since I first read this line
My heart turns into butter still.
"Will you be my Valentine?"

The Mystery of Words

We meet on equal playing fields
We strivers wielding pens;
With timid hopes, exposing thoughts
To candid critic's lens.

The self same words are ours to use
In manner of our choices.
They lay in helpless inert piles
Until we give them voices.

Just as the paint and brush await
The artist's soulful touch,
The notes without composer's skill
Cannot amount to much.

Some have used proud words in prayer
That others use in curses.
We poets take them charily
And turn them into verses.

The marvel of a simple word
And its use never ceases;
The same one found in drivel as
In gifted masterpieces.

If I Were Rich

If I had more than my share of gold,
Ranked favorably with Mr. Gates,
I'd travel forth to see the world,
Try all the lavish foods that sates.
December would find me cruising south
And taking all my friends along..
We'd sail the seas and live in style
And without worry sing our song.

But spring would take me back again
To the snug house he built for me.
I'd walk the boundaries of my land
And give up all thoughts of the sea.
No riches could entice me to
Give up this house he built with love.
We snuggled here for many years
Until God took him up above.

I love each tree he planted for me,
Each blade of grass, so fresh and green.
Most of the year our climate's mild.
The skies are blue the winds serene.
No riches could make me leave my home
Here in the lovely Puget Sound.
My home between mountains and the sea
Lies where I'm always homeward bound.

Lost Summers

I recall when summer
Was sitting in the shade
Drinking icy glasses
Of Mama's lemonade.

In the magic summers
When love was fresh and new;
Delight of summer evenings
Exclusively for two.

Later on the summers
Were two weeks at the shore;
Brushing sand from children
Wishing days were more.

Life with all its burdens,
Halts not for summer's treasure.
There no longer is the time
To taste of summer's pleasure.

Summers have grown shorter
And busier it seems.
Lazy days of summer
Are only in my dreams.

Loved Child

A child who's loved and knows she's loved
Will have a shield to carry her
Through all the troubles life can bring
Through everything that can occur.

A parent's true unselfish love,
Is more precious far than gems or gold;
And though her toys will broken be,
Their love she'll have when she is old.

Arlie with eye of steely blue
Has turned just five years old today.
With love to guide her steadfastly
She has started on her journey's way.

Love she's received is now returned
To ponies, all animals, babies too.
This little blonde's a dynamo
Loves pinks and purples and sometimes blue.

She has a bright inquiring mind,
Learning manners and her ABC's,
With a strong will to carry her
Through little trials and Brothers tease..

This child whose had someone to trust
Will be trustworthy when she 's grown
And generations after her
Will benefit from love once sown.

Whispers In The Night

Rooms whisper in the night time and
Walls echo back their words.
Their voices as melodious
As strange, exotic birds.

I try to understand them, but
They speak in foreign phrase.
I'm taunted by the sounds of night
And quiet of the days.

When you were here to murmur your
Sweet love song in my ear
The walls were blatant listeners
And strained to overhear.

Perhaps they now are speaking of
The way it used to be
When the whispers in the night time
Were love words for you and me.

Who Am I

I awake with the sound of the phone in my ear.
Someone's asking for Stanley, and Stanley's not here.
Who will I be for the rest of my life?
Now that I'm a widow, no longer a wife?

I lie there just waiting for my head to clear,
Looking for courage, defeated by fear.
My eyes open wider, I search for the key,
To find the meaning in this day for me.

I suppose I will shower, and maybe I'll dress,
And then I will have to eat something, I guess.
Then what will I do, that will matter at all?
What's still important? I try to recall.

I pick up the paper, trying to read,
Where are those children that I used to feed?
The husband that used to come first in my life
When I wasn't a widow, but his faithful wife?

The newspaper drops from my useless hand.
Who needs me now? I don't understand,
How a life so fulfilled, has come down to this.
The future's like looking into an abyss.

But there must be more, and I'll have to find it,
My clock has run down, I'll just have to rewind it.
I don't dry my tears, just plan to ignore them,
And turn to my friends waiting there are on the forum.

Shereen and Andrea, AL, Farr and Jill
And all of the rest, my restorative pill.
The tears are now gone, there's a smile on my face.
In this life once so lonely, I still have a place.

War Never Ending

My grandpa was a boy in blue
In the war between the states;
That most disastrous war of all,
Where many met their fates.

It was brother against brother
And mothers prayed for sons
Who met in battle on the fields
With cannon balls and guns.

Grandpa lived to tell the tale,
Proud that he'd won the fight,
To keep his own sons from the job
Of turning wrong to right.

He died in peace while thinking
The scourge of war was o'er,
Not knowing of the big one,
The war to end all war.

My own dad's generation
Paid the price, the world to mend..
They trounced the Kaiser soundly
Bringing that war to an end.

A mere twenty years later
Vile Hitler raised his head
And joined with treacherous allies
To fill the world with dread.

My beloved older brothers
Were called to save the world.
They risked their lives and limbs with pride
To keep our flag unfurled.

Those who came home were hoping
That the world had been set free
For the future generations
From such infamous tyranny.

But then the Korean war broke out
And the one in Viet Nam
Not one of us has ever known
A world of peace and calm.

Our sons and daughters battle
To keep war from our door.
We just keep hoping sometime
We can see an end to war.

To Each His Own

A well known painter stopping by
To take a picture of my yard
Asks me to pose with watering can
Pretending to be working hard.

It's taken almost forty years
To bring my yard to it's fruition.
An artist's painting once well done
Will last for many a generation.

My artistry with spade and hoe
Is never quite a finished work;
Unraveling like unknotted yam
If I digress and duties shirk.

Dear lovely lady do your best
To capture this ethereal beauty,
Blooming now in wild array;
A vivid dish of tutti-frutti.

Next year, perhaps the scene will change.
Efforts to duplicate in vain;
Today's performers in the past
Only your painting will remain.

So why don't I pick up the brush
And cast away my spade and hoe?
The lure of living medium
Only a gardener can know.

Contentment

I've not sailed down Niagara Falls
Nor climbed Mt. Everest heights.
I haven't crossed the Sahara
Or danced under city lights.

I'm just a little country girl
Without the yen to roam.
This lovely bounteous valley
Will always be my home.

In spring the fields of flowers
Call visitors from afar;
Big busses bring some tourists
While others come by car.

Before daffodils and tulips
Have quite faded away
A big expanse of iris
Will brighten up my day.

My children and grandchildren
Love this valley as I do.
Not one has found a better place
To live their whole life through

I'm a few hours from the mountains,
A like time from the sea.
I do not need to travel
The world's right here with me.

Seven Cedars

It was the year of 1954. I was a young woman still, thirty-five years of age, and my children were eleven, nine and going on eight. All were safely in school for seven hours of the day and it was time for me to find a job to help out my husband who had a hard time finding and keeping steady work in these still distressed years after the war.

My younger brother was the Program Director for the local Radio Station, KBRC, located in Mount Vernon, Washington. He told me there would be an office job opening at the radio station soon. The traffic manager was the wife of one of the announcers who had found a job elsewhere and she would be leaving with him.

Hoping my high-school typing skills were still with me, I made an appointment for an interview with the station owner/manager. Somewhat to my surprise, I got the job; one I would keep for thirty years. Those early years of radio and my part in it would make a great story and one I intend to write some day, but radio is not the subject of this tale although there is a connection as you will soon see.

From 8:00 to 11:00 each evening was request time on KBRC. One of the record spinners, Jim Nelly was very popular with the teenagers of the day who kept the telephone lines hot with their requests. Jim was a very enterprising young man, and as radio employees were not highly paid in those days, needed to find a way to augment his income. He devised a scheme to trade on his popularity with the young people of the area. Mount Vernon, at that time, was a small city of around eight thousand people and was surrounded by four or five smaller cities in a twenty-mile radius. These towns nestled in the beautiful Skagit Valley, owed much of their prosperity to the surrounding farms where strawberries and other berries, peas and various vegetables were grown in profusion. The Skagit Valley has some of the richest soil in the world. Many of the younger children earned money for new clothes and entertainment by working summers in the beautiful fields. The indulgent farmers made sure that they did not work too long or hard at their tasks. Indeed the children for the most part, looked forward to these hours in the sunshine and the camaraderie of the other children until the well meaning State Legislature passed laws which great-ly limited this source of labor for the farmers and income for local children. Most of the work is now done by immigrant workers from Mexico.

There was very little entertainment for the children other than school sponsored events, movies and a roller skating rink in the area in those years, so Jim had a plan that he hoped would be a business success for himself and a boon to his young friends. He approached a local bandleader, Harry Lindbeck, who owned a big ballroom on the outskirts of Mount Vernon. Called Seven Cedars for the seven cedars that were growing there at one time, (some of the youngsters re-named it The Stumps). The Seven Cedars building had once been a dairy barn and then a roller rink before being turned into a dance hall. The building was aging but had a beautiful dance floor. Dances were held each Saturday night for the adults of the area but under-age teens were not allowed to attend. I was not privy to the agreement Jim made with the owner of the building but I was included in the disclosure he made to all other employees of the radio station, once his plans were advanced.

He had been given the right to hold teen-age dances every Friday night, from seven to 11:00. He offered several of us a chance to work for him and I was hired as chaperone for the girls. Some of the others would be bouncers and he had several off duty policemen on his payroll. There was a small bar where sandwiches and other foods as well as soft drinks were sold.

The rules were strict. There would be no fighting inside or out and everyone who bought a ticket would forfeit the right to come back in if he went out before the dance closed. Most of the people who worked for Jim were parents of teenagers and we knew how to keep a watchful eye on the attendees.

The dances were a great success from the very first. Seventh and eighth graders up through senior high flocked to these Friday night affairs. If I remember correctly the dances were later changed to Saturday night after the adult dances on that night were canceled.

The dances started out as platter spinning by Jim and others but we soon had local rock and roll bands and some of more renowned playing the popular times of the late 1950's and early 1960's. My youngest daughter, now sixty years of age and a grandmother recalls the wonderful time she had at these dances. She says she wishes she could remember the name of the boy that she used to meet at the dance each Friday, just because they both loved to dance. They did not pursue a relationship of any other kind, just their mutual love of dancing. Some of the popular Rock and Roll bands that appeared were the Drastics, The Dynamics, The Esquires, The Fleetwoods, The Frantics, The Night People, The Swags and one memorable evening the popular Bobby Vinton performed in person.

My children were all young teenagers by this time and none of them ever wanted to miss a Seven Cedars Rock and Roll dance. My son was the eldest of my brood and he was still attending them when a senior in high school and in fact, met his future bride at these dances. I am convinced that half of the young folks of the time met their mate at Jim Nelly's teen- dance.

I lived in the small fishing village of LaConner. Some of the town mothers, knowing I was present at these affairs, allowed their youngsters the first taste of freedom from parental eyes by letting me take them, along with my own, to the dances. Entry fees were just one dollar and affordable even in those tougher times.

These were the days of innocence, before seat belts and strict regulations. I don't know how many young people I crammed into my small car each Friday night but I know it would be far over the legal limit today; and then as we left for home at eleven, they would ask to "drag the gut" through the main street of Mount Vernon. As there were few cars on the streets by that late hour other than other young folks leaving the dance, they had a great time shouting out of the car windows and waving to their friends. I sometimes meet a matronly grandmother, one of those eager teenagers, who speaks of the good times she had at these dances and thanks me for the ride to and fro and for the tolerance I showed for youthful exuberance.

Jim Nelly moved on to a better job at a bigger radio station but the dances did not stop. Randy Craig, our Program Director at the time, took over and I moved up to the ticket sales booth. The kids were still streaming into the dance each Friday night. The younger dancers usually attended the early part of the evening and the older ones came after the various school basketball or football games were over, but order was kept and all obeyed rules. I think perhaps this is the reason that the dances were moved to Saturday night when the building became available for that day of the week. There would be less conflict with the school functions. The far away Viet Nam war was causing some of the recent high school graduates to sign up for service and many of them spent their last carefree hours at this rock and roll dance.

In July of 1962, personal tragedy struck in our family. My husband of twenty-one years, just forty-one years old died suddenly of a heart attack. I was left with two daughters still in high-school (My son had graduated the year before and was working as well as taking classes at the local college) and a very meager income so the dances and the wages I received from them as well as the distraction and comfort from being around my children and their friends when they were having fun, became very important to me.

In the fall of 1963 I was on the job as usual on Saturday evening September 21st, selling tickets for the dance. The popular band "The Dynamics" was playing and the youngsters were having their usual happy time when someone noticed smoke rolling along the floor. My youngest daughter who was now a senior came to the dance on her first date with the boy who would become her husband. They drove into the parking lot well after the start of the dance to find an excited bunch of youngsters standing outside and fire pouring from the building. The adults were busy making sure that every last child was safe before we left the premises. I am proud to report that there was no injury to any child or adult. Some of us did lose our coats because we did not want to tarry too long in the smoke filled room. I had not been particularly worried. I knew there was some smoke, but I expected the fire to be extinguished and peace restored and the dance to continue. I picked up the cashier box of dollar bills and walked out when Randy said it was time to go. Once outside, I turned around and saw that the whole building was ablaze. Only then, did I feel any fear. Avis, my daughter ran up to me, she was afraid I had been caught in the blaze, as she had not been able to find me in the confusion.

We never found out the cause of the fire, but the building was a complete loss. There were rumors that a disgruntled teen who had been evicted for breaking the rules had come back and set the fire. This was never proven and as far as I know, no cause was ever discovered.

Randy did not want to give up this lucrative activity, so the dance was moved to the Moose Club in Mount Vernon and then to a Grange Hall but the magic was gone. The crowds became smaller and smaller and eventually admissions were not enough to pay expenses. The teenage dances were no more than a happy memory.

About Author

I have lived a long life, having been born in North Dakota in 1918. I have survived two World Wars and the big Depression as well as minor wars and recessions.

I was the first daughter of my parents after four husky sons. I was very welcomed by the whole family. My brothers dearly loved having a baby sister. Three years later my sister was born and in 1927 my beloved baby brother came. My folks raised seven healthy and happy children. I left North Dakota in July of 1941 and went to Detroit, Michigan where my betrothed had gone to find work.

We left there in February of 1943 in order to be near my family which had moved to Washington State. My son was born two weeks after we got here. I have lived in the beautiful Skagit Valley in Washington ever since to eventually raise my family, my son and two daughters.

I had never had a job of my own until my children were in school. I applied for a job as traffic manager and book-keeper at my local radio station. I stayed there until I retired at 65 years of age in 1983. Meanwhile, in 1962 after 21 year of marriage my husband had died suddenly and I had been left to fend for myself and children. In 1966 I married a local farmer and we happily built a home on the farm and I have lived here ever since. After losing him, in 1995, I rent my land out to a bulb grower and am surrounded by beauty in the spring. My son died in 1999 and to console my self, I started writing poetry. I have written many, many, poems since, successfully publishing some of them.

Made in the USA
Columbia, SC
12 February 2018